A Day with Librarians

by Jodie Shepherd

Content Consultants

Angela Groth and Marianne Ripin, Ardsley Public Library, Ardsley, New York

Reading Consultant

Jeanne Clidas, Ph.D.
Reading Specialist

Children's Press®
An Imprint of Scholastic Inc.
New York Toronto London Auckland Sydney
Mexico City New Delhi Hong Kong
Danbury, Connecticut

Library of Congress Cataloging-in-Publication Data
Shepherd, Jodie.
  A day with librarians / by Jodie Shepherd.
     p. cm. — (Rookie read-about community)
  Includes index.
  ISBN 978-0-531-28952-5 (library binding) ISBN 978-0-531-29252-5 (pbk.)
  1. Librarians—Juvenile literature. 2. Libraries—Juvenile literature. I. Title.
  Z682.S54 2013
  020.92—dc23   2012013357

Produced by Spooky Cheetah Press

1 2 3 4 5 6 7 8 9 10 R 22 21 20 19 18 17 16 15 14 13

Photographs © 2013: Alamy Images/H. Mark Weidman Photography: 19; Corbis
Images/Gabe Palmer: 20; Getty Images/Andy Crawford/Dorling Kindersley: 27;
iStockphoto/YangYin: 31 bottom right; Media Bakery/Mark Edward Atkinson: cover;
PhotoEdit: 24 (Bill Aron), 23 (Michael Newman); Scholastic, Inc.: 3 bottom, 28, 31 top
left; Shutterstock, Inc./Robert Kneschke: 4, 31 bottom left; Thinkstock: 7 (Comstock
Images), 15 (Creatas Images), 3 top, 12, 31 top right (Ryan McVay), 8, 11, 16.

Table of Contents

computer

scanner

books

Meet a Librarian

Librarians have important jobs. They can help you find a good book to read or some **information** about almost anything.

Here to Help!

Librarians make sure all the library's books are in the right place. That way, people can find what they are looking for.

The librarian can help you use the computer to find information. She can also help you check the online **catalog** to find a book.

If you want to play a math or reading game in the library, the librarian can show you how.

Some children want help with their homework. They can go to the library after school. The librarian knows how to help.

Some adults want to become new United States citizens. They might go to the library to learn about their new country. The librarian can help them do this.

Reading Is Fun!

Everyone enjoys story hour.
The librarian chooses the book.
Then she reads it aloud. Everyone
gets a chance to say what he or
she liked best about the book.

The librarian likes to read.
She knows a lot about books.
She chooses books for the library.

Let's Go to a Library

Some librarians work in school libraries. They might also be teachers. Other librarians work in **public** libraries in towns and cities.

Some people do not have a library close by. Librarians bring the books to them. The **bookmobile** is a library on wheels!

Checkout Time

When a person finds the right book, the front-desk librarian gets to work. First he **scans** the library card.

Then the librarian uses a **scanner** to record which book is being borrowed. She notes when it needs to be returned.

BETHEL
PUBLIC
LIBRARY

Mon.- Wed.- Thurs. 10:00am - 8pm
Tues. - Fri. - Sat. 10:00am - 5pm
Sundays : Sept.- June   1pm - 5pm

The librarian hopes you enjoy your new book. Most of all, he hopes you will visit the library again and again.

Try It! Read page 9 again. Then go to your local or school library and use the online catalog to find a book you would like to read.

Be a Community Helper!

- Visit the library often.

- Try to be quiet at the library. Other people are reading!

- Take care of the books, CDs, and DVDs you take out.

- Return your books, CDs, and DVDs on time.

- If you find a book you like, tell a friend about it!

Words You Know

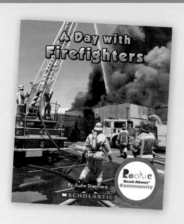

book

computer

librarian

library

Index

Facts for Now

Visit this Scholastic Web site for more information on librarians:
www.factsfornow.scholastic.com
Enter the keyword **Librarians**

About the Author

Jodie Shepherd, who also writes under the name Leslie Kimmelman, is an award-winning author of dozens of books for children, both fiction and nonfiction. She is also a children's book editor.